The S

A Tribu

Edgar B. Madsen

THE SHOESTRING LETTERS

A Tribute to the Immigrant

Fifteenth Edition, 2015

ISBN 978-1-329-33843-2

Acknowledgments

With appreciation to
Dr. Poul Nielsen and his wife, Kirsten,
of Copenhagen, Denmark,
for bringing the Shoestring Letters to us
and then diligently translating them into English

This book was self-published using Lulu (www.lulu.com).
Additional printed copies are available at that site.

Inquiries about the publishing aspect of this book may be directed to:

Ed Madsen
47 McComb Road
Princeton, NJ 08540-1953
EdMadsen@aol.com

The author may be reached at:

Edgar B. Madsen
47 McComb Road
Princeton, NJ 08540-1953

Telephone (609) 924-4017
Email: EdMadsen@aol.com

Edgar B. Madsen has also authored:
Don't You Know Me? A Soviet Prison Camp Survivor's Account

Dedication

In remembrance of my parents:
Niels Boel Madsen   (1897 - 1980)
Dora Signe Jensen a/k/a Signe Boel Madsen (1898 – 1963)

One last visit on the day before leaving for America

With their six-month-old son, Harry, immigrants Signe and Niels Madsen are on the right. Parents Mads Fastergaard and Maren Kirstine Madsen, are seated in front with his sister, Dina. Standing in back are his brothers Marius (at left) and Peder Madsen. For the next thirty years, mail would be the only contact Niels would have with the rest of his family in Denmark.

DET FORENEDE DAMPSKIBS-SELSKAB

AKTIESELSKAB

SKANDINAVIEN-AMERIKA LINIEN

S/S Hellig Olav den 25/9. 1928
2 miles vest for Oslo.

Kære Hjem.

I Dag laa der Brevpapir og Konvolutter
ved hver Kuvert beregnet paa, Jvel, at vi
skulde benytte det til Breve at afsende
fra Halifax, som vi nu nærmer os.
Vi har haft den dyligste Solskin og
næsten stille Vejr under hele Tiden
Havet er næsten hel blank, og vi sejle
c.a. 368 miles i Døgnet. I Spisesalen
hænger et Kort med Ruten, og der bliver
afmærket hver Dag med Flag hvor langt
vi er kommen, og i Morges Aften
skulde vi kunne se New-Foundlands
banken. Vi var kun søsyge det første
Døgn efter Oslo, og da var vi det nas.
ten ogsaa allesammen; siden den
Tid har Turen været en ren Nydelse,
hvis det lykkes at faa Tiden til at gaa
Vi spiser Kl. 7.30 Kl. 12 Kl. 3 og Kl. 6
og Forplejningen er helt ypperlig som
paa et 1ste Kl. Hotel. Vi har Musik
under Maaltiderne og en dyllig Spise
sal at spise i. Hver Eftermidda.
fra 4-5 spiller Orkestret paa Dækket
og saa gaar Dansen —

The Immigrant Experience

Beloved Scandinavian Songs

S/S *Hellig Olav*

The Voyage

Have you ever wondered what it was like for millions of immigrants who ventured across the Atlantic to become Americans? What did they leave behind in their homeland? Was their journey rough? Did they have any regrets? My immigrant parents never spoke about it and, regrettably, I never thought to ask. Now they are gone. Other first-generation Americans say their parents were similarly silent, leaving the same enigma for descendants to ponder.

With relatives visiting from Denmark, we looked for answers at Ellis Island where more than twelve million souls entered our country. At the national monument in New York harbor, you can sense the hopes and hardships faced by immigrants from all over the world. Among many exhibits was one featuring the Scandinavian American Line's *Hellig Olav.*

Many Europeans came to America during the 1920s aboard the *Hellig Olav.* You could sense their hopeful gaiety in photos of immigrants dancing to their own music as the ship carried them across the dark ocean into the unknowable future.

In the evening after our Ellis Island trip, my cousin and his wife handed me a packet of letters, literally tied together with a shoestring. Squirreled away in our grandfather's thatched-roof attic for half a century, they had been written by my parents to their folks back in the old country. Incredibly, one of those letters was written aboard the *Hellig Olav* by my father during their 3,827-mile, 11-day voyage to America.

> *25 September 1928 --"We have had the most lovely sunshine and mostly calm weather during the whole trip. There were almost no waves and we move forward about 368 miles per day.*

The passengers are of many different nationalities. Besides those from all the northern countries there are passengers from Estonia and Lithuania. I just had an interesting conversation with a couple of them. I talked with them about their country but I came to understand that they were pure Bolsheviks. They were of the opinion that it would be better for all the new countries to be under Russia. They were nice educated men who claimed that all the bad things you hear about Russia were merely propaganda and that the morality of Bolshevism was the only right thing.

26 September 1928 -- Today we have had a real storm with the wind howling and the waves passing over the deck. After that we went forward for a few hours with reduced speed because of the fog. They blew the horn every second minute. It is this type of weather which the seamen fear the most because any minute you might collide with another ship or an iceberg drifting near New Foundland.

28 September 1928 -- In about an hour, we will be in Halifax where all those going to Canada get off the ship. We had a gala dinner yesterday evening followed by a ball in the evening until midnight. I played the violin and another played the accordion. We sang "Hils fra mig derhjemme" (Greetings from me to home) again and again. All the people who knew it were singing. Just now we are gliding toward the gangway in Halifax. It is fantastic to see land so near again. In a couple of hours we will go on to New York. Good bye until then.

--Your Niels, Signe, and Harry"

Life in Denmark

Feudalism prevailed in Denmark until the 18th century was drawing to a close. In addition to paying taxes in money and crops, tenant farmers also had to report for work at the manor estate on certain days. Systematically robbed of the fruits of their labor, the farmers simply did not produce enough to carry the nation's economy on their backs.

Finally, in 1788, Denmark abolished the feudal system. After that, life on the farm flourished when the people could own the land on which they toiled. Then, in 1836, Bishop Grundtvig proposed establishment of the Danish Folkehøjskole. By the end of the 19th century, these boarding schools became accessible to the sons and daughters of Danish farmers.

Required by law to provide a general broadening education, folkehøjskoles were expressly forbidden to award marks or grades. The principal task of these state-subsidized schools was to educate students for life. To this day, folkehøjskoles rely on student commitment and teacher motivational skills. For students, it is like attending a college with only one final exam--life itself.

Into the late 19th and early 20th centuries poured the progeny of Danish farm families with their heads full of exciting ideas planted by teachers like Anders Nielsen. One hundred years ago he gave each of the boys in his class a block of wood. Then he said "*Inside this block of wood is a beautiful spoon. Your job is to remove the excess and set the spoon free.*" Among my treasures is the graceful flour scoop set free from one of those blocks of wood by a fourteen-year-old lad in that class.

As my father whittled away on his flour scoop, Nielsen poured a powerful vision into his head, described in a letter on 12 January 1913 to my dad's parents back on the farm:

> *"Today Anders Nielsen told us about America, about Chicago, where he worked as a carpenter. He said that when the train reached Chicago it still took a whole hour to reach the station where we were to get off.*
>
> *When a carpenter had saved $300, then he could buy a lot "on the outskirts" of town, and lumber and bricks for $100. Then he and seven or eight of his buddies would begin building on a Sunday. They would begin sinking 6" x 8" posts into the ground. Then they laid joists and floor on top of the posts. Thereupon they erected 2" x 4"s. At ceiling height another set of joists was laid. Then the rafters, siding and roof. In two Sundays they would have the house built, without losing a single working day."*

Fertile is the mind of a fourteen-year-old. That vision never lost its power. Fifteen years later, my father sailed to America with his young family. Then they rode the train to settle in Chicago. After two decades in America, he would follow his teacher's footsteps as a carpenter. In a few more years his nights and weekends were consumed with designing and building that house "on the outskirts." But it would take a whole lot more than $100 and two Sundays to get it built.

4

The Wider World

In 1914, for reasons little understood by common folk, Europe plunged into a horrific war which claimed more than 8 million lives before the armistice on 11 November 1918. In all probability, the long war was ultimately hurried to its conclusion by the pandemic of 1918. The "Spanish flu," as it became known, killed more soldiers on both sides of the war than all the bullets, bombs, and mustard gas they hurled at each other. Worldwide, the disease killed more than 100 million people in the space of a few months.

The flu's toll was lighter in Denmark. However, concern was clearly evident when my mother wrote home from Askov, where she and her sister Katrine shared a room while attending folkehøjskole.

7 February 1919

"Dear Mother and all of you:

Now it is very long since I wrote, a whole week, but the days go so fast that we just cannot keep up with them. How are you getting along in this terrible cold weather? Can Mother watch it and not let herself freeze and get sick--that we would not like to hear.

I feel good and do not have a cold or anything like that, but Katrine has had a bit of a cold for some days, and today she stayed in bed to bring it to an end. She was planning to get up tomorrow, but I think that would be wrong when the weather is so cold. She has just been rubbed with camphor and drunk chamomile tea, and now she is asleep. She does not hurt in her back or any other Spanish places...."

Then my mother, who was 20 years old at the time, reveals a lifelong love of learning by describing her school day.

"You may believe that I have had a wonderful day. Friday is almost the best one of the whole week. This morning Appel told about the (Danish) constitution from 1865 to 1915. Appel has so much to tell because he himself has moved among Kings, Princes, and Cabinet Ministers. He can come out with delightful stories but his most skillful delivery in the lecture comes in the manner in which he goes over the different paragraphs of the Law.

After Appel's class, I had Dr. Christiansen's class on Danish grammar and composition. Next Biology with Rosenkjaer -- everybody loves his class. Today we heard about conditions required for the soil to be tillable and we saw funny demonstrations with acidic soil and basic soil.

Next it was math with Arnfred, the class for which I am most eager. I think I could do arithmetic from tomorrow until I am fifty without getting tired of it but, unfortunately, we do not have more than three math classes per week. Arnfred has a marvelous method for presenting problems. He teaches math and in the same stroke reviews astronomy, the calendar, and many other fields.

After lunch, World History with Christiansen. You have heard no end of praise for him, and he deserves it too. We read about ancient Greece and Rome but it does not get to be dull for we see every little event in relation to what has happened in the Nordic countries through the years, or to what is happening in Europe today. Right now I am happy to be here this winter rather than the winter before because then the world lay in a ruin of which there was almost no beginning or end in sight. Now, on the other hand, the turmoil is over with at least to some extent. I am sure that we will hear more of the viewpoints of the different nations, and about where we must go from here, and what really was the jolt which started the war.

From 4 PM to 5 PM we have anatomy and hygiene. Next gymnastics. And this evening's historical lecture by Christiansen was about Poland. We have had several delightful lectures about the Catholic Church. Now I finally know what kind of a figure the Pope is. I have never known that before, only surmised it. Nor have I known the Catholic Church as well as I do now.

I have so often thought that it looks like we went to a very good elementary and advanced school in our little town of Hurup. Even here, where there are so many learned heads, I am not altogether left behind in Natural History, Chemistry, Astronomy, and Anatomy. But on one point I am ignorant, namely in World History. I believe that it is a great wrong that we never laid eyes on a book like that in our Hurup school. And you can believe that my arm is not among those two or three which are raised when the teacher wants to see how many here have never studied World History. I keep silent and read it over one more time in our room.

Many greetings to Father, Mother, and all.

--Signe"

How she would have relished another year of folkehøjskole. But her father decreed: "enough was enough!" A year later, she was working as a housemaid at Thon, a farm in Smaalenene, Norway, southeast of Kristiania (Oslo). From there she wrote a birthday letter to her 12-year-old kid brother.

"Dear Little Arne: *8 February 1920*

*Many, many congratulations with your birthday today. Lately I
have been so very, very busy. Of the eight of us here in the
house, seven have had the Flu and they are far from being over
it yet. I am the lucky one who up to this point has gone free.
But for that reason I have been really hard pressed, taking care
of the household, the chickens* and the patients. It is quite
wearisome to hustle upstairs with my 63 kilograms (139 lbs.)
innumerable times during the day.*

*It started with Agnes, she became indisposed about two weeks
ago, since then she has been in bed, and could eat nothing, only
drink fruit juice. Then she slept for three days and had no food
at all. On Saturday Mrs. Dingstad became ill...could not hold a
glass when she would drink. It is really strange how they all
sleep when they are ill. They wake up, ask for fruit juice, and
ten minutes later they are again asleep, sometimes for two
hours, sometimes several hours whether night or day, and when
they wake up again they cough much.*

*Mr. Dingstad and the others are so nice to me. He adjusted the
skis so I could use them but I did not have time. I had baked
crackers and was cooking goat milk cheese. There was lots of
cream so I really should have been churning butter also. But in
spite of everything I put on the skis and went out for half an
hour to satisfy myself and the others. You can understand, Arne,
that I did not forget your birthday, but I have plunked myself
into bed as soon as I was done for the day, sometimes at 10 PM,
sleeping through until 6 AM. Greetings to all,   -- Signe"*

---

* Those chickens may have been the problem. Nearly 90 years
later, virologists concluded the deadly 1918 pandemic was caused
by an avian virus transmittable from birds to humans. The family
at Thon was likely sickened by a somewhat less virulent avian
strain. Fortunately for them, my mother was apparently immune.

Family Life

Huge families were the norm in Denmark during the nineteenth century. About the time my mother was born in 1898, her grandmother was asked if she had many children. She said "No." Later when it came out that she had nine children, her interviewer exclaimed: "Nine children! How can you say you don't have many children?" She countered: "*Nine isn't so many. My mother had seventeen and my husband's mother had nineteen!*"

My mother was the third of nine surviving children. As soon as they were able, the six girls and three boys pitched in on farm chores. Mom attended folkehøjskole in Denmark when she was twenty before working in Norway and England as an au pair. Then she returned to wait on tables at Volk Mølle, the farm her father had purchased. With a picturesque mill pond, it was perfect for a summer restaurant where young singles, my parents among them, could meet.

As good as life was in Denmark, farming was fraught with market risk. An attempt to restore the Gold Standard in 1927 pummeled the export of butter and bacon. It crushed Denmark's dairy and hog farmers. Dad was one of them. Furthermore, the land could hold only so many people. With successive generations of nine or more children, moving away loomed as a necessity.

In those days before television, family singing was a staple of Danish family life. They were good songs about their country, nature, and God's care for each of us. One is a beautiful lullaby known as *Evening Star*.

> *Evening star up yonder,*
> *teach me like you to wander,*
> *willing and obediently*
> *the path that God ordained for me,*
> *Evening star up yonder….*

My mother's older sister, Katrine, was the first to leave for America. On the night before she left in 1920, the family listened quietly at Volk Mølle as Katrine sat at the piano and played one favorite melody after another. Then another, lingering lovingly until she struck the final note. Everyone knew that this was to be the last one. The next morning, the entire family went to the rail station to see Katrine and her husband, Niels Sloth, off on their way to the United States...to Chicago. Her mother never saw either of them again.

Within a decade, Katrine was followed by her youngest brother and three sisters, one of whom was my mother. They all settled in Chicago and were, for the most part, isolated from Denmark for decades by an ocean, a Depression, and a war. But the Chicago contingent gathered frequently for holiday and birthday celebrations. On those occasions, Katrine's daughter, Lillian, would play *Evening Star* and the other beloved Danish songs at the piano. Today, Katrine's descendants number more than sixty, spanning the continent from Alaska to Florida.

The Bjerre Bunch

While driving across windswept Jutland in 1999, we came upon some whimsical pottery perched on a roadside sign which said: "Bjerre Keramik." Turning into the driveway, we found a farm where part of the barn had been converted to the manufacture and sale of ceramics. As we looked at the merchandise, it became apparent that the owner, a woman a few years younger than us, did not speak English.

In limited Danish I managed to communicate to the shopkeeper that my middle name is "Bjerre" (rhymes with "Berra" pronouncing the "j" as "y"). Her eyes lit up and she asked: "What number are you?" I responded: "1450" and asked, "What number are you?" Her reply: "1499." Then she ran into the house and returned with the family book in which we are numbered. It established we have the same great-grandmother, Madame Bjerre, the legendary matriarch and teacher who did not have "many" (only nine) children.

There were also nine children in my mother's family. Although surnamed Jensen, they bore the indelible stamp of their mother's lineage. She was a Bjerre. With more than its share of educators, entrepreneurs, and engineers, the Bjerres are an independently minded and voluminous tribe. About four hundred of them get together every third summer for a family reunion in Jutland. With more than 4,000 names, the family book has given way to CD-ROM and Website *(www.Bjerre.net)*. Sadly, it records that Maja, the youngest girl, died in 1944 in Holland "under krigen" (in the war).

Back row: Katrine, Bertel, Jens, Signe, Karen, Elisabeth
Front row: Ellen, Maja, Arne

If you look closely at the photograph taken in 1912 of my mother and her siblings, you can see that the oldest boy, Jens (age 12), stands with his right shoulder high and arm curved. That is because there is a crutch under his arm. One day his mother brought the boy's shoes in for repair. The cobbler said, "These shoes cannot belong to the same boy; the left one is badly worn but the right shoe is hardly worn at all." It turned out that several weeks earlier, Jens had been butted by a goat and the wound had become infected. Then, with gritty determination he favored the leg, keeping his injury a secret until it was too late. As a result, Jens stomped through the rest of his life on a wooden leg earning him rejection at Ellis Island. It was America's loss!

Returning to Denmark, he designed sophisticated machinery and went on to manufacture exquisite parquet flooring. About her brother, my mother said, "Jens was clever; he could have built a pyramid!" He was also a shrewd businessman, claiming, "It does not matter if prices are going up or prices are going down. So long as prices are changing, I can make money!"

Standing ramrod straight is Bertel (age 10), who also had engineering ability and a good business mind. On farms throughout Denmark today, you will see silos bearing the name of the company he founded, "Assentoft Silofabrik."

The youngest boy, Arne, emigrated to America at the age of twenty. Before attaining his civil engineering degree, he explored the southwest via Greyhound bus. On one occasion, he dawdled too long inside the depot where the bus had stopped for ten minutes. Arne emerged from the building to see the bus already more than 100 yards away, picking up speed. Rather than do nothing, he started chasing after on foot. Just then the bus stopped at a railroad crossing awaiting an approaching train, long enough for Arne to catch up with the bus and his suitcase.

For the rest of his days, Arne lived true to his conviction that "The biggest difference in the world is the difference between something and nothing!" Yet "for everything there is a season." At age 91, as he lay on the operating table during his final illness, Arne looked up at the surgeon and said: "If the bus leaves the station, don't chase after it."

Four of his sisters emigrated to America, settling in Chicago. Karen, the oldest, cultivated the finest Danish cultural traditions. Nearly a century later, her descendants promote Danish folk dancing and crafts at exhibitions in the Midwest.

Elisabeth, born in 1901, worked for the rich and famous as a masseuse and cook. Once, when she was giving a massage, the woman exclaimed with admiration, "Where did you ever get such strong hands?" Lis replied: "From milking cows!"

Lis walked everywhere. While working as a cook at an estate about five miles away, she would walk over to our place for a short visit and return on foot. At the age of 79, she fulfilled her lifelong dream. Beginning at Gedser on the German border, she started walking north and kept on walking, *for the entire length of Denmark!*

Nobody paid any attention when Lis started her trek, a distance of about 240 miles. But reporters were there with photographers as Lis cooled her feet in the surf at Skagen, where the North Sea collides with waters from the Baltic at the Danish peninsula's northern tip.

Ellen, the second youngest girl, outlived all of her siblings. During our visit in 1999, she treated us to afternoon coffee in the third floor walkup apartment where she lived independently in Copenhagen. A delightful soul at age 93, she told us that she had just registered for her customary fall class in gymnastics!

Danish Primitive Gymnastics

There are no parallel bars, rings, or balance beams. No judges. No scores. Hence, no losers. Everybody wins because instead of competition, the emphasis is on improving each participant's physical health. A better word to describe it would be "calisthenics," which is derived from two Greek words, *kalli* meaning "beauty" and *sthenos* meaning "strength."

The concept is simple enough: programmed group exercise is the most efficient and least tiring way to restore our muscles, of which there are more than 600, to proper function. Some muscles tend to be too short, others too long, still others too weak. A well-trained instructor knows how and when to direct students to stretch, pull, and strengthen. Forty minutes of nonstop exercise need not be exhausting. To eliminate fatigue, the instructor directs students to exercise one part of the body, say the arms, while the legs are at rest. Later on the legs get a workout while the arms relax.

The foremost proponent of Danish Primitive Gymnastics was Niels Bukh (pronounced "Book"), who founded the Ollerup Academy of Physical Education in 1920. Its objective was to train gym instructors who would then return to their respective home communities and teach youth to strive towards goals of self-improvement--physically, mentally, and morally.

The Ollerup Academy has graduated more than 20,000 instructors. To direct specific exercises, they are trained to reduce the number of words to a minimum. And they give instructions for the next exercise while the students are still busy doing the preceding one. Then, upon cue, the students shift to the next exercise without interruption. This economizes time and retains the benefits of gradual increase in tempo and intensity of physical exertion.

Advantages of this system are many. A single leader can direct the exercise of a large group. Classes numbering 20 to 40 students are common. The exercises promote strength and agility. Free movements are easily adaptable to individual body peculiarities. Expensive apparatus is unnecessary and attendant exposure to liability for related injury is obviated.

Where public or private schools are strapped for funds, the economy of this effective physical fitness delivery system is obvious. One wonders why we Americans have not demanded this kind of physical education in our schools. Perhaps our schools don't know about it or how to do it.

For information on the 4-month International Youth Leader (English speaking) Training Program, check out: *Academy of Physical Education, Ollerup, Denmark - YouTube*.

Ellis Island

One out of every three living Americans can trace his or her ancestry back to someone who entered through Ellis Island. Seduced by tales of easy wealth, what immigrants sailed into was a hard life. Oft quoted is the lament: "They told me the streets were paved with gold but when I got to America, I found the streets not paved at all and they expected me to pave them!" Still they came, by the millions, mainly through that little patch of land in New York harbor.

By the time Ellis Island immigration activity ceased on November 11, 1954, twelve million immigrants had passed through the gateway. It has been called "the island of tears" because records dating from 1900 show that over 3,500 people, including more than 1,400 children, died on Ellis Island. On the brighter side, 355 babies were born there.

After immigrants were ferried from their ship to the island, they climbed to the second floor Registry Room under watchful eyes of U. S. Public Health Service doctors at the top of the stairs. That is where Uncle Jens was rejected because of his wooden leg. But they let him ride around Manhattan in a taxi before shipping him back to Denmark. Years later Jens lamented: "Had it not been for my wooden leg, I would have jumped out of that cab and run away so fast they never would have caught me!"

For many, like Uncle Jens, that doctor's mark on their coat meant the difference between "America" and "Going back." Sometimes families were torn apart; a parent on one side of the ocean leaving a spouse or child stranded on the other. Steamship companies, obligated to absorb the expense of deportees as a cost of doing business, carried as many as one thousand a month back to Europe

To mediate this maelstrom of grief, confusion, and jubilation (for the lucky ones), the Ellis Island staff included interpreters. One of them, fluent in Croatian, Italian, German, and English, was a law student who served from 1907 to 1910. He surmised untold anguish could be avoided if immigrants were examined in their home country rather than at Ellis Island. Finally on May 21, 1924, the requirement for completing physical and mental examinations *before* embarking on the voyage was signed into law. (Ten years later the interpreter who championed that reform, Fiorello LaGuardia, was sworn in as mayor of New York City.)

Prior to the Immigration Act of 1924 and the earlier Emergency Quota Act of 1921, shipping companies profited from low fares to illiterate passengers who were crammed into squalid dormitories below deck called steerage. But the 1924 Immigration Act required literacy. Consequently, the passenger lines were confronted with a higher level of clientele who could no longer be enticed into squalid steerage conditions. Therefore, ships were refitted with modest cabins to accommodate fewer, but higher paying, passengers.

After 1924, the voyage tended to be more like a cruise. About life on board the ship my father wrote, *"The food is always as good as in a first class hotel and we have music during the meals in a lovely dining room."* Although my parents did not know it at the time, that 1928 voyage would prove to be the most elegant vacation of their lives.

In all, 99,414 Danes passed through Ellis Island between 1892 and 1931. But my parents were not among them. Like most immigrants after 1924, they came with visas in hand, pre-qualified in Europe, thus bypassing the island of tears.

Culture Shock

Thorvaldsen's Christ

The culture my parents left behind was rich in literature and the arts from luminaries like Thorvaldsen the sculptor, story teller Hans Christian Andersen and theologian Kierkegaard who said: *"To venture causes anxiety, but not to venture is to lose oneself."* In the 20th century, Isak Dinesen (Karen Blixen's *nom de plume)* wrote *Babette's Feast* and *Out of Africa.* Into the 21st century Victor Borge, the zany Danish concert pianist, regaled his audiences. Explaining how to distinguish a viola from a violin, he quipped: "A viola burns longer!"

On the streets of Copenhagen a man on horseback mingled among the people. His name was Christian X, King of Denmark. When my parents arrived in 1928, they found Chicago also had a king. He rode the streets in a bullet-proof limousine; his name was Al Capone.

Murders were an everyday occurrence as Capone and rival gangs battled for control of gambling, prostitution, and bootleg liquor. Chicago would endure 115 bombings in 1928. Violence peaked in 1929 with the St. Valentine's Day massacre in a warehouse ten minutes from where my parents were living. Seven members of the rival Bugs Moran mob were gunned down by Capone's hit men dressed in police uniforms. No one was ever convicted of the crime.

How do newcomers negotiate an alien culture like this? They look for gatherings of people who speak their language. In those days, every nationality had a place like that. Danes flocked to the Danish American Athletic Club where the customary greeting was *Velkommen herhid* ("Welcome to this place") and they could get a lead on a job or housing. Occupations provided colorful nicknames like those of the plumber, "Drip-Drip Petersen," elevator repairman "Up-and-Down Larsen," and "One-way Larsen" the undertaker.

Incorporation of Chicago's Danish American Athletic Club (DAAC) in 1923 coincided with the post World War I peak in westbound passengers carried by Scandinavian American Line ships. Sufficient numbers of Danes poured into Chicago during the 1920s to support purchase of a clubhouse near Humboldt Park where gymnastics, folk dancing, and good times flourished for the next quarter century.

Following the end of World War II in 1945, the club celebrated Mother's Day on May 12, 1946, with a "Welcome Home" banquet and dance at the Edgewater Beach Hotel. Five women and seventy men were honored for their military and merchant marine service. Sadly, the honor roll that night included two "gold star" sons killed in battle.

The DAAC reached its peak that night at the Edgewater Beach. Soon, most of those seventy-three returning service men and women would leave town. First, off to college on the GI Bill. Then, on to suburbia.

20

The Great Depression

Although written more than fifty years ago, it is as if the letters from my immigrant parents were mailed last week and arrived this morning. The emotions they express plummet and soar like a ship tossed on the ocean's mighty waves.

Things had not gone well with their dairy and hog farm in 1927. Years later Dad would blame the (falling) price of pigs for driving them out of Denmark in 1928. By June of 1929, eight months after their arrival in America and four months before the stock market crash, he was riding high on optimism.

> *"In five years we may be citizens in the US and can come home for a visit...."*

But from depths of the Great Depression in February, 1933, he wrote:

> *"This winter we have had very little income. It is very seldom that we know from where we shall get money for food for the next week, but we have got it until now."*

Thirty years later, on the eve of our wedding, Dad presented us with a poem which begins:

> *"How strange it all seems to see him prepare*
> *for a home of his own--with his sweetheart to share.*
> *One cannot help but pause to review*
> *and attempt to imagine what's in store for the two.*
> *Will their journey through life be nearly as tough*
> *as that of his parents--because that has been rough...."*

From what little they had, my relatives shared much. For two years while going to college, Uncle Arne bedded down each night on the couch in my parents' living room. His meals were provided at the boarding house of my "Moster" (Danish word for "Mother's sister") Karen. When Arne and the boarders finished eating each evening,

Moster Karen's children were dispatched with leftovers to Moster Katrine's, where their five cousins were flirting with starvation.

Then, in 1934, a rich man in Lake Forest placed a classified ad in the *Chicago Tribune* offering free rent in exchange for farming and light carpentry skills. In response, my parents packed their belongings and 6-year-old son into an old car and drove nearly 1,000 miles due south to Mobile, where they spent two years as tenant farmers.

On their first afternoon in Alabama, following a rain, they walked the boundaries of the farm. The next day a neighbor introduced herself and, by and by, asked if it was my mother and father she had seen walking around the field on the previous day. When my mother said "Yes," the neighbor said "Oh, that was very brave of you." Puzzled, my mother asked what was so brave about that? The neighbor replied, "Weren't you afraid of the water moccasins?"

Deadly snakes were not the only problem. True, the house had electricity, central heat and indoor plumbing. But none of it worked. And Dad felt the owner did not hold up his end of the bargain with promised farm equipment. In the end, my father was able to grow the crops but could not get them to market. Due to a dock strike, he had to watch the fruit of his labor rot. It was hardly a level playing field.

Before returning to Chicago in 1936, my parents stood before an Alabama judge to be sworn in as citizens of the United States. Mom could barely understand the judge's southern drawl so my father answered all the questions. That was fine. But there seems to have been a little misunderstanding. To this day, my parents' citizenship papers declare they have sworn away all allegiance to King Gustav of Sweden. Not very hard for Danes to do!

On their last day in Alabama, my parents and their 8-year-old bade farewell to dear friends at a Sunday School picnic. Seventy-five years later my brother recalled it as the day they ate his pet chicken for lunch.

Passport to Employment

Perhaps it had fallen out of a box being shoved aside at an earlier time. I really don't know. But its sudden appearance in our attic a decade after my father's death was a bit spooky. It was almost as if his ghost had passed through and dropped the little flat wallet on the floor where it was sure to be found.

What emerged from the wallet was my father's fifty-year-old passport to employment--his Local #3 membership card in the International Hod Carriers & Building Laborers Union. Toward the end of the 1930s, as Chicago haltingly emerged from the Great Depression, union membership became a prerequisite for employment. Yet, even with a union card to land a good job like mixing concrete by hand, Chicago's bitterly cold winter weather could throw a man out of work.

"Dear Everybody: *December 11, 1937*

Yes I think that it has been a long time since I wrote you. As time goes on, I find it less interesting to tell you about our rather stormy life. Each time you think that you have started something on which you can continue to build, something else happens to interrupt the process and you have to start all over again.

For the last two or three months I have hardly earned anything. It seems as if we are to have another Depression and maybe one which is worse. Without anybody knowing why, all the large factories suddenly lay off thousands of workers. Those who lose their jobs lose their ability to buy. Those who are working keep what they earn because they are afraid of losing their jobs as well. *

A week ago, however, I succeeded in getting work at the construction of the Humboldt Park Armory which will take most of a year to build. But then the cold weather stopped us. We mixed concrete when the temperature was 11 degrees above zero and had heating under the heaps of gravel and sand. But when the temperature got down to 8 degrees above zero, work stopped because it was too cold for the concrete. We earn $1.02½ per hour, 40 hours a week, which is good pay. By the way, my boss is a fellow Dane named S. N. Nielsen. He constructs buildings for several million dollars each year. He will turn 80 years of age next January but is working like a man of 45.

Best Regards and Merry Christmas"

In a postscript, my 39-year-old mother announced they were expecting another child sometime around Easter. She was sure it would be a girl this time. But I wasn't!

———

* Economists still debate whether the culprit was fiscal policy (introduction of the Social Security payroll tax at the beginning of 1937) or monetary policy, blaming the Federal Reserve for nipping recovery in the bud by prematurely tightening the money supply later in the year.

The War Years in Denmark

In 1938, my 72-year-old Bedstefar (Grandfather) Jensen sailed from Denmark to visit us in Chicago where five of his nine children lived. A few months later he headed home on one of the last crossings before U-boats started sending ships to the bottom of the Atlantic.

Shortly after Germany forced Denmark to sign a non-aggression pact on May 31, 1939, Victor Borge outraged the Nazis with his sarcastic observation: *"How nice. Now the Germans can sleep in peace, knowing that they will not be invaded by us."* But when there is war, the first casualty is truth. On September 1, 1939, falsely claiming that Germans in Poland were victims of a bloody terror, driven from house and home, Hitler unleashed blitzkrieg (lightning war) against Poland. No matter that Denmark was a neutral nation; on April 9, 1940, claiming he was there to "protect" the nation, Hitler sent his troops into Denmark.

To this day, from Denmark's beaches along the North Sea, you can look up along the bluffs and see the remains of concrete bunkers built by Denmark's uninvited protectors. The German war machine wanted to repel any invasion of the Jutland peninsula by Eisenhower's Allied forces. They also wanted local cooperation. But the Danes had other ideas.

Apocryphal, perhaps, but illustrative of Danish spirit is the story about the flag. During the occupation, a Danish soldier emerged from the palace, lowered the swastika and raised the Danish flag to its rightful place. Incensed, the German commander sent a man over to replace it with the German flag and deliver a note to the palace saying that the next man to lower the swastika would be shot. Not long afterward, out from the palace strode the King with the Danish flag under his arm to do the deed himself. They did not dare shoot the king!

Then there is the tale about Hitler sending the King a congratulatory telegram, wishing him a happy birthday and looking forward to the day when Germany and Denmark would be one big fatherland. The King is said to have wired this reply to Hitler: *"Thank you very much for your birthday greeting and good wishes but Denmark is really all I can handle."* One enduring myth is that the King wore a yellow star of David in solidarity with the Jews. In truth, the King never put on the star because Jews were not compelled to do so while on Danish soil.

Americans lived with wartime price controls and rationing of gasoline, meat, and sugar. But Danes endured much greater deprivation. Uncle Marius, who lived in Jutland, developed cancer which required weekly radiation therapy at a hospital 75 miles away. But his tires were no good and new tires were restricted on account of the war. However, because of his urgent medical need, the authorities granted him special permission for new tires. That made it possible, once a week, for Uncle Marius to ride 75 miles to the hospital, undergo his radiation treatment and ride 75 miles back home, on his bicycle!

Danish protection of Jews is undeniably one of the war's brightest chapters. As the High Holy Days were approaching in 1943, word leaked out that the Gestapo were about to round up all Danish Jews for deportation. On Rosh Hashanah, two days before Nazi persecution of Danish Jews would begin, the following pastoral letter was issued to churches where it was read to congregations throughout the land.

> *The Danish bishops have on September 29th, this year, forwarded the following communication to the leading German authorities through the heads of government departments:*
>
> *"Wherever Jews are persecuted as such on racial or religious grounds, the Christian church is duty bound to protest against this action:*
>
> *Because we can never forget that the Lord of the Christian Church, Jesus Christ, was born in Bethlehem of the Virgin Mary according to God's promise to His Chosen People,*

Israel. The history of the Jewish people before the birth of Jesus contains the preparation for the salvation God has prepared for all mankind in Christ. This is shown by the fact that the Old Testament is a part of our Bible.

Because persecution of the Jews conflicts with that recognition and love of man that are a consequence of the gospel which the church of Jesus Christ was founded to preach. Christ is no respecter of persons, and He has taught us to see that every human life is precious in the eyes of God. (Gal. 3:28)

Because it conflicts with the concept of justice which prevails in the Danish people, settled in our Danish Christian culture for centuries. In consequence of this, equal rights and responsibility before the law, and freedom of religion, are secured to all Danish citizens according to the words of the constitution.

We regard religious freedom as the right to worship God according to vocation and conscience and hence that neither race nor religion can, of themselves, deprive any citizen of rights, liberty or property. Despite differences of religious opinion, we will struggle for the right of our Jewish brothers and sisters to preserve the same liberty that we prize more highly than life itself.

The leaders of the Danish Church are fully aware of our duty to be law-abiding citizens, who do not set themselves up against those exercising authority over us, but at the same time we are in conscience bound to assert the law and to protest against any violation of it. Therefore we shall, if occasion should arise, unequivocally acknowledge the words that we should obey God rather than Man."

Signed on behalf of all Danish Bishops

H. Fuglsang Damgaard

27

During the next three weeks, a flotilla of Danish fishing boats spirited seven thousand Jews across the water to safety in Sweden. When they returned to Denmark after the war, it is said many found flowers waiting on the table to greet them in their homes which had been maintained by neighbors while they were away.

While the war was still on, the Germans never were able to silence a pirate radio station operated by Danish resistance from a fishing boat somewhere in the Atlantic. At a concert celebrating the war's end, Victor Borge evoked tumultuous applause with his rendition of the song played on Pirate Radio after Hitler's propaganda broadcasts by Joseph Goebbels: Gershwin's "It ain't necessarily so."

An end to the German occupation was announced by British Viscount Montgomery over the BBC at approximately 8:40 PM on 4 May 1945. After international mail service was subsequently restored, one of my father's cousins sent us several tiny photographs taken the next day in a nearby town. Cryptic captions inscribed on the back of each picture speak volumes about the German occupation which Denmark and its freedom fighters had resisted for more than five years. To Danes old enough to remember, the Fifth of May is revered as Liberation Day much like America's Fourth of July.

On 5 May 1945 the German commandant in Skjern is stopped by a freedom fighter on the motorcycle.

German soldiers on 5 May showing up to surrender their weapons. Do you see that freedom fighter with the machine gun? It is loaded with real bullets!

"So gehen wir nach Deutschland" (title of a German song which means: "So, then we go back again to Germany") Look at the vehicles! This was a common sight on Danish roads after capitulation in May, 1945.

Refugees in railroad cars. When Germany capitulated on 5 May, we had about 250,000 refugees in Denmark.

29

Seven Danish-American immigrant cousins in 1929
(All five boys were destined for wartime military service.)

The same seven cousins in 1960 after the boys had all returned home.
In civilian life, from left to right, lawyer, secretary, school principal,
customs officer, rocket scientist, nuclear physicist, and secretary.

The War Years in America

A family gathering for the fifteenth birthday of my cousin, Lillian Sloth, will never be forgotten by anyone who was there. In the middle of it, somebody rushed in the door with the news that Pearl Harbor had been bombed. It was December 7, 1941. Soon her older brothers were in uniform. Art drew stateside duty in the Army. Harry, a Navy hospital corpsman attached to the Marines, survived the horrors at Saipan, Tinian and Iwo Jima.

Uncle Arne put his Danish ingenuity and American Civil Engineering degree to good use. At the Prairie Shipyard in Seneca IL, he supervised construction of LSTs (Landing Ship Tanks), inventing more efficient ways to weld hull plates. Designed with a nearly flat bottom, the bow of LSTs flopped open to disgorge tanks and troops for landings. While the war was still on in 1945, my cousin Sven and I stood next to dignataries on the shipyard platform where we watched our Aunt Ella, Arne's wife, whack a bottle of champagne across the bow to launch one of the 157 ships constructed on that former farm in Seneca. To my astonishment the LST, longer than a football field, slid sideways, rather than backwards, down the launching ramp before splashing into the Illinois River, then on to the Mississippi and Gulf of Mexico before serving 20+ years in Okinawa, Korea and Viet Nam. Whatever it was Uncle Arne did for the seams on that hull, it withstood the test of time

On the home front, to help with the food supply, Victory Gardens became a common sight on empty lots all over Chicago. Apartment dwellers, like us at the time, could stake out a vegetable garden, no questions asked. It was the patriotic thing to do.

After the war, my cousins all returned from military service. The Sloth boys went to Grand View College in Iowa on the GI Bill. Art became an elementary school principal. Harry settled in a career with the United States Customs Service. Their older brother, Eric, who had graduated third from the top of his 1,300 member high school class, returned from the Navy to become a nuclear physicist.

Chicago's Melting Pot

If ever there was a melting pot of cultures, it was Chicago in the 1940s. Bordering the stockyards on Chicago's south side, worker housing filled neighborhoods kept immaculate by women who would emerge with babushkas on their heads, broom in hand. A little to the north, frugal Czechs flanked Cermak Road where it seemed there was a Savings and Loan at every other door...with a bar in between. The Irish dominated City Hall. Scandinavians shared neighborhoods with more numerous Germans, Polish, and Italians.

In 1948, when I was almost ten, my father ended a letter to his family in Denmark bragging, *"Edgar has got a newspaper route. He delivers 60 papers a day. Sunday morning he has to get out of bed at 4:30 a.m. This is the best thing that has happened to him for a long time."* The *Chicago Tribune* dragged me out of bed on Sunday mornings. While delivering the *Chicago Daily News* on weekdays I would pass a building with a sign which proclaimed: *"Honor the Dead by Serving the Living."* It made sense to me then. It still does today.

On Wednesdays, I tossed the *Chicagovski* on doorsteps of Polish subscribers. In those days, the Polish population of Chicago outnumbered that of Warsaw. With names like Pappas, Pishke, and Wu, my Chicago Public School classmates revealed the cultures from which they were emerging. After school on Mondays, Alexander Pappas would hop on a streetcar heading for Greek school. On Wednesdays Raymond Pishke and the other Catholic kids got out of school early for catechism class taught by the nuns at St. Philomena's.

On holidays I spent many happy hours playing Monopoly in the back room of a Chinese laundry owned and operated by the hard-working parents of my school chum, Richard Wu. (Wheeling and dealing with that Monopoly real estate apparently left its mark on our psyches; Richard became an architect and I wound up appraising commercial properties including one on Pacific Avenue, not far from the Boardwalk in Atlantic City.)

Meanwhile at the "world's busiest corner" in Chicago's Loop, Mom waitressed in the Carson Pirie Scott department store lunch room. With a winning smile throughout life, rather than borrow or do without, she would "get a little job." In the summer of 1948, she wrote back to Denmark about her 12-day "vacation" in Door County, Wisconsin, a place she had wanted to visit for years. Dad was too busy and she did not drive, so she took the train and had a great time.

> *"It was a big treat to relax from my daily work. Niels did not have time to go so he gave me $50 and wished me a good trip. I could have stayed in a boarding house at $35 per week but I wanted to use the time to see the country and learn about the ways and customs. So I took work on the biggest farm and picked cherries. It is so beautiful to ride across the fields. I could pick 16 buckets the first day and 34 the last. It takes 10 buckets to pay for board; lodging is $2 per day.*
>
> *Door County has only one bus per day which goes north and one which goes south so if you haven't got a car it is almost impossible to see some of the surrounding area. Therefore the last week I was there I chose to sort cherries in the evening from 7 PM until 3 AM. Then I got up at 9 AM and hired local people to drive me around to the most beautiful places including the Ellison Bay School of landscape architect Jens Jensen.* -- Signe"*

———

* Superintendent of Chicago's Humboldt Park circa 1900, *Danish-born* Jens Jensen (1860-1951) encouraged a connection for everyone with plants native to their environment, coining the term: "living green." In 1904 Jensen proposed preservation of Chicago's lakefront and river lands. Today's Forest Preserves west of the city and magnificent parks bordering Lake Shore Drive are his legacy. Jensen's 128-acre Ellison Bay property has been preserved and is now home to The Clearing, a not-for-profit corporation, offering a variety of summer classes in the Danish Folk School tradition and workshops throughout the year.

Post War

It must have been a tremendous relief to my mother when the war ended in 1945 while my brother, Harry, was finishing high school. Nevertheless, he soon joined the peacetime Army. After Basic Training, he signed up for Officer's Candidate School (OCS). Somehow the orders got fouled up and Harry was stuck for awhile in a barracks with other OCS enrollees, awaiting their orders *and* pay.

With time on their hands and little money, the soldiers hit on a novel plan. They agreed that everyone in the barracks would contribute all their money to a common pool. Then they would draw lots so that the winner could take all of the money in the pool, just enough for him to buy one movie ticket! But he had to recount the movie's plot to his barracks buddies....

After 90 days, Lieutenant Harry B. Madsen emerged and, in due time, received orders to Korea (before the Korean War). Early in 1948, Dad wrote:

> *"Harry came home by plane for Christmas, was at home for almost 3 weeks, then flew to San Francisco from where he will soon be sailing to Korea. It turned out that there was more time for him to wait for the boat than he had expected, so he started exploring California. Yesterday we got a letter that he had bought a house! Yes, a house with windows and doors. It will be built during the year he stays in Korea, and his agent will arrange for leasing the house. No help needed from his old man. No Sir. No advice needed either. He did it all on his own with his own money and credit, and he does not let himself be cheated like his father...."*

There was a glitch, however. Harry was old enough to go to war as an officer and a gentleman but he was not yet 21 years of age. A minor in the eyes of California law at the time, he was too young to own property! The deal fell through.

One morning later that year, while Harry was on active duty in Korea, orders came down from Headquarters transferring 10% of the men out of his Company. They were replaced the same afternoon by soldiers from a previously all-black outfit. Implementation that day of President Truman's Executive Order 9981, which abolished racial segregation in the Armed Services, led our nation into the post-war civil rights era.

In those five brief years between the end of World War II and 1950, other momentous changes were reshaping our culture as well. Television sets made their appearance in furniture store windows on their way into living rooms across America. Returning veterans set the wedding bells ringing. At the peak in 1945 and 1946, a single church in Chicago could have as many as a dozen wedding ceremonies (an hour apart) on a single day. Like the proverbial pig in a python, the ensuing baby boom has been working its way through our economy ever since.

Cars, cars, and more cars carried families like ours out of the cities into the suburbs. In 1950 my father, then working as a carpenter, bought a building lot for $1,200. Or so he thought. It turned out that he had actually purchased the front halves of two lots. Before he could get a building permit, he had to buy the back half of those two lots, for $1,300. In March of 1951, we moved into the suburban house he had been designing and building for nearly a year. A single-story ranch, replete with Formica kitchen counters, knotty pine paneling inside, and cedar shakes outside. Now, half a century later, when we come upon an occasional house with similar features, it almost invariably dates from the early 1950s.

Suburban Life

The city we left behind had houses with tiny yards on streets laid out neatly in a grid running east/west and north/south, with occasional jogs to correct for the earth's curvature. In the suburb to which we moved, sprawling lawns and meandering lanes were the norm.

There were 46 students in my Chicago 8th grade grammar school class where we did not learn much grammar. Transferring into a suburban 8th grade class of 27, I was dumbfounded when the teacher asked a spelling bee winner to name the form of speech for the word he had just spelled. I can still remember David Bigford's answer: "It is a verb intransitive." But to this day I haven't the foggiest idea of what a verb intransitive is.

Born in the worst of times, when the world was staggering out of the Great Depression into the cauldron of war, my new classmates and I spread our wings in the best of times. We were too young for service in World War II or the Korean War (into which my brother was recalled for a second tour). Our High School Class of 1955 graduated in a year of Eisenhower's presidency during which not one American died in combat anywhere in the world. Our town was a place where the wealthy nestled on gracious estates under a leafy canopy by the water. They called it Lake Forest.

Education in those days meant a healthy balance of the "three As"-- Academics, Athletics, and the Arts, including domestic and industrial. Somehow they made it possible for a student preparing for college to learn how to sew a dress and cook a meal or fix a washing machine and a leaky faucet. It was also possible for an athlete so inclined to be in the band, sing in the chorus or act in plays such as "Our Town" on the school stage.

None of our class was numbered among the rich, for whom most of us boys had caddied. We were children of the working class. Our parents were gardeners, custodians, policemen, farmers, and railroad workers, including Gary's dad, who was a conductor on the trolley line linking our town with Chicago, one hour south, and Milwaukee, one hour north.   David's father fixed refrigerators.   My dad was a carpenter. Mom worked as a waitress and cook.

When called to serve, Dad proudly donned a white carnation in his lapel to usher at the First Presbyterian Church of Lake Forest where the middle and upper classes rubbed shoulders on Sundays. Midway through worship, with brimming offering plates in hand, ushers would form two abreast before marching down the aisle to the strains of *We Give Thee But Thine Own*.   On one of those Sundays, the usher at his elbow was none other than the owner of that land in Alabama which Dad had farmed in leaner times.   Now they marched on level ground at the foot of the Cross, rich man beside the man who was no longer poor.

The suburban environment also afforded my father an opportunity to heed the voice proclaimed by Isak Dinesen's Babette.   That voice within the heart of every artist which cries: "Give me a chance to do my very best!"   Pictured wearing overalls in front of a half-built house, my dad scrawled on the back of photos sent to Denmark in 1955:

> *"This is Dr. North's house under construction.   It is 69.5 feet long (garage included) and 30 feet wide.   Basement under the whole house.   Together with another carpenter I did all the carpenter's work in less than 900 hours (60 working days).   The house cost a bit more than $25,000. It is situated on one of the posh streets (Sheridan Road). The site is 100 feet by 347 feet.   The first load of lumber arrived on June 29th.   The family moved in on October 8th.   I got 5% of the total price as general contractor which was $1,250 on top of the pay I received per working hour of course."*

Although addressed to his father and brothers, you can almost hear my dad shouting back across the span of forty years to Anders Nielsen, the teacher who gave him the vision of building a house on the outskirts of Chicago.   *"Here I am, Anders, I did it!"*

38

Trinity Danish Lutheran Church

Located a few blocks south of Humboldt Park, directly across from Chicago's Norwegian American Hospital, stood Trinity Danish Lutheran Church. The ship is what stands out in my memory from infrequent visits to the sanctuary where I sat clueless through services conducted in Danish. Like the Danish church pictured, it had a model ship hanging from the ceiling with its bow pointing toward the altar. Years later I learned the ship's significance was its representation of life as a journey which will bring each of us to one of two ports....

A treasure from that church is the music, preserved by a far-sighted group of American-born youth of Danish descent. In the 1940s they started translating Scandinavian hymns and folk songs. Then, with a force not even they imagined, Danish congregations throughout the land disintegrated in the suburban migration after WW II. Few churches remain in America where services are still conducted in Danish.

The last time I drove by Trinity Lutheran Church in Chicago, the sign out front said "Iglessia Lutrano Trinidad." I do not mourn for the loss of Danish worshipers. To the contrary, I pray God's blessing on the latest wave of immigrants and would bid them "*Velkommen herhid.*"

39

Niels & Signe Madsen in 1959
at *Mockingbird Hill*, their home in Lake Forest, Illinois

A New Dance

When my parents came to America from Denmark, an old violin tagged along on their journey though life. In Alabama, where they toiled with the soil during the Great Depression, Dad would lift his violin from its dusty case for special occasions like a church picnic. Later in Chicago, hands callused from shoveling concrete in bitter cold would draw the bow across tightened strings to make melody for Danish folk dancers.

Sometimes on a quiet evening at home, with the distant gaze of a mother nursing her child, Dad would lean back in his chair and coax *Hils fra mig derhjemme* from deep within the old violin. The melancholy song portrays a lonely sailor, far from home, urging birds winging overhead to carry his love and greetings (*Hils*) "from me" (*fra mig*) "to home" (*derhjemme*). "*Hils* to father, mother, sis, and brother...."

After some years, American folk music crept into the repertoire. Soon, *Red River Valley* led the hit parade at our house. Then midway through the twentieth century my folks took up square dancing. They were not alone. Americans from all walks of life were promenading in western garb to the cadence of square dance callers accompanied by down-home music.

In short order my father progressed from dancer to caller, with mom assisting to demonstrate dance maneuvers. He also enlisted three Swedish immigrant pals as backup band. Thus, improbable as it sounds, violinist Walter Johnson, accordionist Gustav Frederickson, and Ruben Olson on guitar (carpenter, gardener, and plumber by day) became *The North Shore Rangers* by night, led by N. B. Madsen, the square dance caller with a Danish accent. Only in America!

42

Back on the Farm

In my Bedstefar (Grandfather) Madsen's farming community of Faster, so the story goes, there lived a boy whose parents feared would come to nothing. It seems the sixteen-year-old dreamed only of becoming an artist. Such a waste! In the hope of imparting some practical skills to their young dreamer, his parents sent the boy to live with Bedstefar Madsen for a while so he could learn how to raise chickens.

Things must have looked pretty dismal when young Ole arrived. The old farmhouse where Bedstefar lived was deteriorating, in part because of holes which storks had pecked in the thatched roof. Furthermore, my grandfather was 88 years old at the time (in 1955). But it was not long before the lad persuaded Bedstefar to pose for a few minutes while the artist in residence sketched a charcoal portrait. It captured the old man's character with incredible clarity.

Fortunately, attempted transformation of the fledgling artist into a chicken farmer was an unmitigated failure. The boy, Ole Alkjærsig, continued to pursue his love of art until he became one of Denmark's leading restorers of art treasures.

Meeting my grandfather in Denmark was at the top of my bucket list after completing military service in 1961. He was still living on the farm with my father's younger brother, Uncle Peder. The two of them got into a heated conversation during my first visit. In broken Danish I said: "Grandfather, when you speak, you talk with your hands, just like my father." The old man grinned and said something which Uncle Peder translated into English: "Grandfather says to tell you, we are not angry; we are just arguing!"

43

Uncle Peder was a hunchback who lived out his three score and ten as a bachelor. He told me that when he was 16 years old, he left home to start a world revolution. I asked, "What happened?" He replied: "It was a shame; I caught a cold!"

Hiding behind that mask of humor was a deep disappointment revealed in papers left behind after Peder died. He, too, had hoped for a new life in America. Correspondence in 1928 refers to his appointment at the Consulate where, we surmise, his application for a visa was rejected because of his crooked spine. Like their ancestors, Bedstefar and Uncle Peder lived out their lives on the farm. But they were the last. Before selling the farm after Peder died, the family came upon letters bundled with a shoestring in the attic under the thatched roof.

Thus ended one family's bond with the land memorialized on 15 July 1925 at dedication of a monument on the Faster family farmstead with the following words etched in granite:

> *Times come and times go.*
> *Families come and families go.*
> *For two hundred years on this piece of land*
> *The same family has made its stand*

Danish Americans

The floodgates of Danish emigration to America were opened when the U.S. Homestead Act of 1862 offered free land to settlers. Initially farmers were attracted to Midwestern states. Later, Danish colonies flourished in Chicago, New York, Omaha, Racine, Minneapolis, and San Francisco.

Through the years, about 400,000 Danes sought a new future in America. One of them, Max Henius, emigrated to the USA in 1881, finding success in Chicago. To celebrate Danish-American heritage he founded the Rebild Festival, held each July 4th since 1912 except during the two world wars.

Surrounded by flags for each of the fifty states, thousands gather on the heather-filled hills of Rebild National Park in Denmark to celebrate U.S. Independence Day and the immigrant ties which bind Denmark to America. The annual program includes music, folk dancing, and speeches by dignitaries, world leaders, and celebrities. Rebild speakers have included Richard Nixon in 1962, Victor Borge in 1976 and Garrison Keillor in 1991.

When we were there in 1982, we heard America's beloved coloratura soprano, Beverly Sills, tell about her experience growing up as a first-generation immigrant. Born in Brooklyn, she recalled living in a one-bedroom flat where she shared the bedroom with her parents while her older brothers slept on a hide-a-bed in the foyer.

To preserve Danish-American history, Rebild's founder also created the Danish Emigration Archives in Aalborg on the web at *www.emiarch.dk*. Resources in America include The Danish American Archive and Library on the web at *www.danishamericanarchive.com* and The Museum of Danish America, 2212 Washington Street, Elk Horn, IA 51531 (*www.danishmuseum.org*).

Mount Rushmore's National Memorial is our most prominent creation by a Danish American. The massive 60-foot-high heads of George Washington, Thomas Jefferson, Abraham Lincoln, and Theodore Roosevelt were sculpted from 1927 to 1941 by Gutzon Borglum, whose father was a Danish immigrant.

Finding Themselves

Until the day she died, Mom praised my father's victories and stood by him through one failed business venture after another. A carpet cleaning business in the 1930s came to naught. After the war he manufactured wood diving boards with twenty-six laminations so they would not break. But they did. His kitchen cabinet shop in the 1950s was short lived. He tried mightily to promote noncompetitive physical education for our schools. But America was not yet ready to listen in 1963 when he sponsored a tour by 28 Danish Gymnasts from the Ollerup Academy of Physical Education.

In his later years, Dad loved to tell the joke about a hippie who went to Europe to find himself..."but he wasn't there!" Hearty laughter after every telling of that tale said something about the immigrant predicament. Many came in search of themselves. Who among us has not similarly searched?

For my father, it took fifteen years from the day he set foot in America before his first sighting of himself. It happened in 1943 when he enrolled in a Dale Carnegie public speaking course. My mother later recalled Dad's praise for that course was the first good thing he had to say about America.

When his classmates cajoled him into writing the class song, they unleashed a talent for transforming narrative into verse. (Previously he had claimed inability to make two lines rhyme.) Turning to the tales of Hans Christian Andersen, his rendition of *The Tin Soldier* in verse begins:

> *Once upon a time, so the story runs,*
> *there were twenty-five soldiers with sabers and guns.*
> *Their uniforms were red with shades of blue,*
> *to be sure they were quite a formidable crew.*

They were brothers in arms, believe it or not,
for all had been cast from an old tin pot.
Tin soldiers, you see; and here we begin
to relate what can happen to a man made from tin....

During his final illness, with my brother's encouragement, Dad compiled a little book of his favorites. He was to see the galley proofs but final copy did not return from the printer until the day after he died. The last page reads: *"I, the author, being an immigrant (trying to find myself) hereby conclude this little collection of poems and rhymes by paying tribute to the immigrant.*

The Immigrant

If I were a sculptor with talents and skill
I would add to the Rushmore creation
Of the Founding Fathers on a Northern Hill
'The Immigrant' who built up this nation.

I would picture him as 'The Wanderer'
                         forever on his way
Towards places where the pastures are greener.
He is never at ease, seldom happy and gay
But vigilant, for his senses are keener.

I would picture him struggling in a ceaseless quest
For places in the sun where it shines.
I would build him a monument and leave it to rest
On a rock among northern pines.

                    --N. B. Madsen"

BELOVED

SCANDINAVIAN

SONGS

EVENING STAR

Carl Mortensen

As a lullaby

Eve - ning star up yon - der, Teach me like you to wan - der will - ing and o - be - dient-ly The path that God or- dained for me! Eve-ning star up yon - der!

50

EVENING STAR

Evening star up yonder,
Teach me like you to wander,
Willing and obediently,
The path that God ordained for me!
Evening star up yonder!

Teach me, gentle flowers,
To wait for springtime showers,
In this winter world to grow,
Green and strong beneath the snow!
Teach me, gentle flowers!

Teach me, lonely heather,
Where songbirds nest together,
Though my life should seem unblessed,
To keep a song within my breast!
Teach me, lonely heather!

Mighty ocean, teach me,
To do the task that needs me,
And reflect, as days depart,
Heaven's peace within my heart!
Mighty ocean, teach me!

Shady lanes, refreshing,
Teach me to be a blessing,
To some weary soul each day,
Friends or foes who pass my way!
Shady lanes, refreshing!

Evening sun, descending,
Teach me, when life is ending,
Night shall pass and I, like you,
Shall rise again, where life is new!
Teach me, sun descending!

--Christian Richardt, 1861
Translated by S. D. Rodholm

SPLENDID ARE THE HEAVENS HIGH

Splen-did are the heav-ens high, Beau-ti-ful the
ra-diant sky, Where the gold-en stars are shin-ing
And their rays to earth in-clin-ing, Beck-'ning us to
heav'n a-bove, Beck-'ning us to heav'n a-bove.

SPLENDID ARE THE HEAVENS HIGH

Splendid are the heavens high,
Beautiful the radiant sky;
Where the golden stars are shining
And their rays to earth inclining,
 :: Beck'ning us to heaven above. ::

It was on the holy night,
Darkness veiled the stars so bright;
But at once the heavens hoary
Beamed with radiant light and glory,
 :: Coming from a wondrous star. ::

When this star so fair and clear
Should illume the midnight drear,
Then according to tradition,
Should a King with heavenly mission
 :: Unto earth from heaven descend. ::

Sages from the East afar,
When they saw this wondrous star,
Went to worship and adore Him,
And to lay their gifts before Him,
 :: Who was born this midnight hour. ::

Him they found in Bethlehem,
Yet He wore no diadem;
They but saw a maiden lowly
With an infant pure and holy
:: Resting in her loving arms. ::

Guided by the star, they found
Him whose praise the ages sound.
We, too, have a star to guide us,
Which forever will provide us
:: With the light to find our Lord. ::

And this star as bright as day,
Which will never lead astray
With its message so appealing,
Is the Word of God, revealing
:: Christ to us as Lord and King. ::

-- N. F. S. Grundtvig   Translated by J. C. Aaberg
from *Hymnal for Church and Home*

I SAW HIM IN CHILDHOOD

Smoothly

Norwegian Folk Melody

I saw Him in child-hood with eyes bright-ly beam-ing, At home in the hills where the sun-light was stream-ing; We play'd with the stars, on the clouds swift-ly rid - ing, And saw not the cross which the wood-lands were hid - ing.

54

I SAW HIM IN CHILDHOOD

I saw Him in childhood with eyes brightly beaming,
At home in the hills where the sunlight was streaming,
We played with the stars, on the clouds swiftly riding,
And saw not the cross which the woodlands were hiding.

I saw Him in youth when my soul was unfolding,
My spirit flew high when His glory beholding;
He beckoned my soul, and He filled me with gladness,
His glory lent brightness to life's gloom and sadness,

I saw Him in manhood, when Adam resembling,
My soul for His righteous judgment was trembling,
When dimmed were my eyes and my vision was darkened,
 Since unto the tempter my spirit had harkened.

First then I could call Him my Master and Savior,
First then I could look on the cross as a favor,
First then I could give Him my downbroken spirit,
In life and in death to rely on His merit.

Since then I have told Him, to Him I will hurry
With weeping my face in His bosom to bury;
Since then I have asked Him with mercy to guide me
And in His pavilion securely to hide me.

To Him I will hasten, His name softly calling,
When broken and weary my house shall be falling;
I'll greet Him with joy when my heart ceases beating,
And unto His kingdom my spirit is fleeting.

--Vilhelm Birkedal
Translated by P. C. Paulsen
from *Hymnal for Church and Home*

Der er et Bibliothek med Bøger til
Udlaan, og hver Eftermiddag faar vi
en lille Avis trykt om Bord med de
sidste Telegrammer fra Danmark
og America. Om Aftenen gaar Dansen igen paa Dækket i Maaneskin.
2 Gange om Ugen forevises der levende
Billeder i Spisesalen. I det hele taget
gøres Rejsen saa behagelig som mulig
for Passagererne. Rejseselskabet er
af mange forskellige Nationaliteter
foruden fra alle de nordiske Lande
er der Passagerer fra Estland og Litau-
en. Jeg har lige haft en interessant
Samtale med et Par af dem. Jeg talte
med dem om deres Land, men jeg
forstod efterhaanden, at de var rene-
livede Bolchevikier og var af den
Mening, at alle de nye Lande var me-
get bedre tjent med at være Vasal-
stater under Rusland. De var pæne,
dannede Mænd og de hævdede bestemt
at alt det daarlige, man hørte fra
Rusland var Propaganda imod
Rusland, og at Bolchevismens Moral
var det eneste rigtige. Den allerstørste
Del af Passagererne talte jo mer eller
mindre engelsk, og det er en stor

Oplevelse at tale med alle disse
Mennesker, som kommer fra Alverdens
Kanter.

den 26/9.

I Dag har vi haft rigtig Storm med
Tuden og Søernes Raken ind over Dækket.
Efter det sejlede vi nogle faa Timer
med sagtnet Fart i Taage. Der hylede
i hvertandet Minut med Taagehornet
Det er det Tøj, Sømændene er allermest
bange for, da man i hvert Øjeblik
kan møde et andet Skib eller
Isbjerge, som findes her omkring
New Fundlandsbanken. Nu er Taa-
gen igen lettet, og i Nat skulde vi
passere Spidsen af New-Fundland,
og saa nærmer vi os jo Maalet.
         Harry har været rask hele
Tiden og opholder sig om Dagen paa
Dækket i sin Vogn. Har Underhold-
ning hele Tiden, saasnart han er vaa-
gen –. Der er altid nogen, som interes-
serer sig for ham. Han har sin egen
reserverede Stol under Maaltiderne
og bliver vartet op af Tjeneren med
Kiks og Servietter, eller hvad der
kan interessere ham –.

Den 27/9.

Om en Times Tid er vi i Halifax
hvor alle de, som skal til Kanada
stiger i Land.
Vi havde Festmiddag i Aftes og
Bal i Spisesalen til Kl. 12
Jeg spillede Violin og en anden spillede
paa Harmonika.
Hils fra mig derhjemme blev gentaget Gang paa Gang acompagneret af
Sang fra alle som kendte den.

———

Just nu glider vi til Landgangsbroen i Halifax. Det er ligefrem
en stor Oplevelse at se Land igen
saa nær.
Om et Par Timer glider vi videre
til New-York.
Farvel saalænge

Eders Niels og Signe og Harry

Gaardejer

Mads Fastergaard Madsen

"Norway" Astrup

Skjern

Danmark